Grounded: Life Lessons

Mark Winn

Winn, Mark, Grounded: Life Lessons
Copyright 2018 by Mark Winn
Published by KWE Publishing
Front and back cover photograph from www.canva.com
Front cover & page 13 illustration by Jared Mason
ISBN (second edition paperback): 978-0-9997254-3-6
Library of Congress Control Number: 2018952127

The suppositions expressed in this manuscript are solely the suppositions based on the research and inferences of the author and do not represent the thoughts or opinions of the publisher.

Second Edition. All rights reserved. This book may not be reproduced in whole or in part without written permission from the publisher, except by reviewers who are hereby given the right to quote brief passages in a review. No part of the publication may be reproduced or transmitted in any form or by any means, electronic, mechanical, photocopying, recording, or otherwise without prior written permission from the publisher. Although every precaution has been taken to verify the accuracy of the information contained herein, the author assumes no responsibility for any errors or omissions. The author shall have neither liability nor responsibility to any person or entity with respect to loss or damage caused, or alleged to have been caused, directly or indirectly, by the information contained in this book.

(Formerly The Chickens Will Tell On You!!! Farm Life Lessons: Wisdom About Family, Life and Living)
(ISBN (paperback) 978-0-9997254-2-9)

Acknowledgements

I am highly appreciative of all the people who have planted seeds of growth in my life. My father used to say, "People don't have to be nice, and when they are, they don't have to be nice to you." To all the people who have contributed to my life, thank you! I would also like to acknowledge my wife and children who inspire me to always climb higher.

Contents

Introduction	1
Chapter 1 What Do Farmers Go Through?	5
Chapter 2 Why Would An NFL Player Go Into Farming?	9
Chapter 3 The Chickens Will Tell on You!!!	13
Chapter 4 Wisdom Mind vs. Emotional Mind	17
Chapter 5 Being Rooted	23
Chapter 6 The Potential Is in the Seed	27
Chapter 7 Why Did I Start Farming?	33
Chapter 8 Allowing the Fields to Recover	39
Chapter 9 It's Time for Market	43
References	49

GROUNDED
Life Lessons

Introduction

When you think of all the things that impact our lives, what is one of the best examples that can teach us lessons about finances, personal growth, work ethics, and problem solving? The answer is farming.

Farming is used to teach economic classes examples concerning supply and demand. In finance and personal growth, it teaches us about planning and delayed gratification. In work ethics, it teaches us to put the work in first and continue to labor towards yielding a harvest. In problem solving, it teaches us to deal with our problems and work through them to resolution. There are so many attributes we can learn from farming.

But when you look at our lives, we totally run in the opposite direction. We don't plan with our finances or personal growth, and we seek immediate gratification in all things.

We have developed a mentality that says, "tomorrow will take care of itself and I deserve to have it all now!" Whether you work for yourself or someone else, we often look to find the shortcuts to the top. Now there is nothing wrong with finding the shortest road, but the reality is that the shortest road doesn't teach you enough. Mentors in farming, whether they are other farmers or family members, provide wisdom. Following their wisdom gets you where you need to be but ignoring their advice always ends to your detriment.

In our personal lives, we don't try to work through our relationships anymore. We don't cultivate and develop them; we just ask, "what is in it for me?" We are always looking for the quick fix in weight loss or the fastest meal because "I don't have time to plan". We give up easily and justify why we don't continue to work towards a harvest

Strawberries that are grown naturally are red all the way through. A strawberry that is white inside or even hollow doesn't last as long because air space or oxygen inside the fruit increases the speed of decay.

that can vastly improve our lives. And we are not willing to work through problems. We avoid, dismiss, discount, or blame others for our problems.

Farming makes you handle life and deal with its storms. Farmers look at trends in weather, productivity, and the economy to make it. Farmers plan for success and deal with the heartache and cost of getting there, no matter how long it takes. They don't create multiple exit plans because they are often working towards a legacy for their families. In many ways, we can look at the attributes of farming as excellent life lessons to be applied to both our business and personal lives.

So why do we sometimes buy strawberries at the store that are white inside? The company producing the strawberries sends them out before they are ripe but sprays a chemical that turns them red by the time they reach the store. The result is they are not as healthy as the naturally grown strawberry nor as delicious. It is the same in life.

Please note, we are not talking about farming corporations. We are talking about family farms that have sustained themselves for the centuries or have developed into a business that serves our communities as well as the legacy of the family.

The focus is on lessons that help us serve. One vital thing with farming is that by using the best methods learned, we all benefit from the harvest. For example, managing the soil to keep micro-organisms intact provides major benefits to your crop. Is this not the same way in our lives? Every time we continue to create quick fixes, produce more for less, cure disease with something that creates more side effects than the disease itself, etc., we don't improve our lives. We make them more challenging, artificial, and unhealthy, and generations suffer for it.

Why are we less happy, healthy, and prosperous than ever before? This doesn't mean people aren't doing well, but overall as a world, we allow ourselves to be further influenced in the wrong directions. The principles of farming are some of the oldest in time, but a principle ignored is a principle not used.

Why do we have economic turmoil in business, world economies, and our personal finances? Is the answer greed with short cuts, lack of planning, and only thinking about the next win that is going to save the day by betting your future? Does any of this sound relevant to what we face?

The adage, "learn from your past mistakes and you won't repeat them" doesn't seem to be

The purpose of this book is to help us to look at ourselves and our behaviors through farming. Farming has been around since the beginning of civilization and there is so much it can teach us. You will read interesting facts and anecdotes from time I have spent with experienced farmers and often their families. The idea for this book came from my experiences as a risk advisor working in agribusiness as well as my love for the life lessons martial arts uses in real life for personal development. You will find there are ideas with which you are familiar but aren't applying to your life in business, personal growth, and health. To receive the most from this book, you will have to set time to meditate on what you have read. Otherwise, it will be another gloss-over event in your life that you can say you did but didn't receive a lifelong benefit.

This is also not a quick-fix book. Just like farming, you must show the tenacity to develop and cultivate change in your life to reap the harvest down the road. And just like true farming, if you reject the chemicals and artificial methods to produce something, you can develop a healthier and more beneficial life.

Visiting Browntown Farms in Warfield, Virginia, I was given a pint of strawberries and tried a couple on my way home. They were so good I took my foot off the gas! I had never tasted strawberries so good and knew this is how they should taste. I felt robbed after all these years of getting strawberries at the store. Fortunately, more of these strawberries can be found in local grocers but you have to look for them.

In business, you may bring a product to market for less only to find that someone will bring it for even less than you have. The public believes it is all the same until the value in products and services are no longer there, then they move on to the next best thing.

In personal growth, whether you are pursuing higher education, developing a relationship, or trying to be a better you for yourself and others, a quick fix without learning and developing the experience won't get you where you want to be with a new foundation.

If you have just gone through the motions, having hit or miss behaviors, they are not a part of your core. If you just worked to get the paper/degree/certification, finish a checklist, or give yourself a pat on the back without applying the experience to your life, you are just fooling yourself and it will show in everything you do.

In health, you say "I don't need to sleep, I have work to do, I hate water, I need something quick to eat, I don't have time for exercise because I'm too busy." And the solution you choose is a drink to lose weight or keep you awake, a pill to lose weight or counteract other medications from health issues you have caused for yourself, or a workout video that you won't be able to find in six months and will say, "it doesn't work."

We often say we don't like drinking water because we have programmed ourselves to prefer other things, but no one is born hating what is so vital to our existence! The healthier alternative is getting proper rest, choosing to drink water, and planning out your day for meals and activities that will keep you healthier with more energy and a productive life.

The strawberry is just a small example of how this book can change your perspective by looking at farming as a way of life. Obviously, not everyone will stop their profession to start physically farming. But, seeing the principles of farming as a way of life can make you proud of your life and happier.

Let's start this journey by looking at what farmers go through and how it can apply to our lives.

Stop and smell the strawberries! Considered members of the rose family, they give off a sweet fragrance as they grow on bushes.

Chapter 1
What Do Farmers Go Through?

How do the issues the farmer faces size up to the problems and issues faced by the general population?

Farmers' Challenges

What happens when your crops are ruined by fire, disease, weather, loss, or change in economic demand if you are a farmer?

Well, first let me tell you, they can't just "fold and quit." They are too invested in time, cost, and commitment. They do what is necessary to recover, limit the damage, rebuild, and grow.

At this point, let's look at how the general population handles these situations in life. We first and foremost quit and say, "it's not worth it." But this is not just how

Did You Know the Following People Grew Up on a Farm?

- Miley Cyrus – Musician
- Eva Langoria – Actress
- Charlize Theron – Actress
- Taylor Swift – Musician
- Carrie Underwood – Musician
- Jewel – Musician
- Jennie Garth – Actress

we react in business situations. We react this way with weight loss and other areas of health, marriage, relationships, managing financial ruin, and making a comeback. And in most cases, this is due to not being as invested and committed to the right things, and then saying to yourself, "I'm done."

Okay, how do the issues the farmer faces size up to the problems and issues faced by the general population?

I met a vegetable farmer at a conference who was elaborating on what a keynote speaker had discussed. It had to do with animals stealing and eating her vegetables.

She first noticed the loss in her fields and had to stop the "bleeding" or loss of vegetables by investigating. It was happening overnight, so she ended up camping out to solve the crime. She was willing to spend several weeks in the fields to disrupt this pattern of loss. That's commitment! Are you "bleeding" but willing to do nothing? Does that show commitment?

We need to use this example in our lives by investing in our own lives. She didn't know what the cause was right away, but she was willing to invest her time and attention to solve the problem because it impacted her livelihood. Too often, we just move on to the next thing. We take such a "pay toilet" mentality with everything. "This business plan doesn't work, forget about it" or "This marriage doesn't work, get a divorce" or "I haven't been good at tracking my finances; don't bother because I'll always be broke." We can only change this pattern with investment and commitment.

I had a friend who was a barley farmer, and he decided to partner with someone who would be able to get his barley into beer inputs production. The partner not only failed to come through, but basically fled owing my friend money. He had to burn the barley which was valued over $150,000. How would your world have looked that day? How many people you know would have recovered from a loss like that? How would it have impacted your relationships at home or with your family?

Would your family have said to quit and find something else to do? Would your spouse blame you for financial ruin?

Would your business partner recognize it as a business loss and move forward or justify that they did all the right things and say it was your fault? Farmers have no alternative but to keep pressing forward because of their investment and commitment.

Chapter 2
Why Would An NFL Player Go Into Farming?

You're making the biggest mistake of your life, said Jason Brown's agent. To which he said, "No, I'm not!"

About Jason

When you hear about NFL players, you usually hear about records they set or trouble they've gotten into. You don't really hear about all of those players who are well-grounded. Often, you just know they live a life of excess. Knowing of players who give back to foundations and nonprofits lets you know some of them do have a community connection and are not all flash. So players definitely give but we don't hear as much about it. You never know how they impact other lives. You see the glory but you don't hear the story of how they got there.

In the previous chapter, we listed a number of celebrities who grew up on farms. Another person we didn't mention on that list is Jason Brown. Here is more information about Jason:

Did you know this about Jason

| He holds four state championships in track and field North Carolina: Three in Discus and One in Shotput

| Along with Chris Spencer, he was considered one of the best centers available in the 2005 NFL Draft

| The deal between the Rams and Jason Brown made him the highest paid center in the NFL in 2009

Exceling in both football and in field and track, Jason Brown was raised in Henderson, North Carolina. In addition to being a gifted athlete, Jason was a member of the honor society.

During his career at the University of North Carolina, Jason didn't miss a single game. At UNC, he was a tackle, then a guard, and later moved to center for the last three years before he graduated. His success at UNC made him one of the most coveted centers during the 2005 NFL Draft. In 2005, he was selected in the fourth round of the draft by the Baltimore Ravens.

Jason played with the Ravens from 2005 until 2009. When he was eligible as a free agent in 2009, he was considered by many to be the best interior offensive lineman available. The Los Angeles Rams NFL football team was so impressed with Jason that they offered him a deal worth $37.5 million dollars over a five-year contract. This deal also included a $20 million dollar guaranteed money agreement. This amazing deal made Jason the highest paid center in the NFL when it was approved on March 12, 2009.

Jason was 29 years old when he made the decision to leave his career in football. Why? He wanted to become a farmer.

When Jason contacted his agent about his career change, his agent said, "You're making the biggest mistake of your life," to which Jason replied, "No, I am not."

At the time he made the choice to leave the NFL, Jason had no experience as a farmer. He shared that he learned about farming practices in 2012 by watching YouTube videos.

Jason has a farm in Louisburg, North Carolina, called First Fruits Farm. At First Fruits, Jason grows sweet potatoes and cucumbers. His passion extends to local food pantries to whom he has donated over 46,000 pounds of sweet potatoes and 10,000 pounds of cucumbers.

"When you see them pop up out of the ground, man, it's the most beautiful thing you could ever see," said Brown. He said he has never felt more successful.

"Not in man's standards," said Brown. "But in God's eyes."

But God cares about the NFL, right?
There are people praying to Him on the field all the time. "Yeah, there's a lot of people praying out there," said Brown. "But, when I think about a life of greatness, I think about a life of service."

See, his plan for First Fruits Farm is to donate the first fruits of every harvest to food pantries. "It's unusual for a grower to grow a crop just to give away," said Rebecca Page, who organizes food collection for the needy in North Carolina. "And that's what Jason has done. And he's planning to do more next year."

Brown has 1,000 acres, which could go a long way toward eliminating hunger in his neck of North Carolina. "Love is the most wonderful currency that you can give anyone," said Brown.

Why am I spending time sharing Jason Brown's story with you? Because anyone who has heard him speak as I have has been highly inspired by him. So often we attempt to measure success by popularity, property, finance, and celebrity. When Jason speaks, you can tell he is concerned about the values and life lessons he is teaching his five children. Often there is no better training ground for faith and family than a farm. It strengthens our values, work ethic, and appreciation for life.

Too often in our society today, children are not being taught responsibility because we have taken all responsibility from them outside of school. They don't have to tend to anything, raise anything, and in some cases earn anything because of their family's income. Much of what they have is given to them. This can include details such as lack of attention to general hygiene that can continue into adulthood.

But how grateful are we in this condition? How much easier is it to develop depression, become a bully, and wallow in low self-esteem when we base things on what we see (television, social media, behavior modeled in school) instead of developing them through what we do?

Someone who has been through life experiences is always better able to deal with the future than someone who hasn't. Without coping mechanisms built on past experience, we flounder or mimic what we see. Now going through something can be a task, direct training, or working through a problem or a failure. It is the challenges in our lives that make us better and stronger. If you look at any nation or civilization through history, you will see there was some challenge that was overcome that raised their people to another level. Sometimes these challenges were natural, some were born out of tragedy, some out of war, some out of a desire to step up to the next level, but no matter what it was, it was meeting the challenge that raised them.

Chapter 3
The Chickens Will Tell On You!!!

Chickens are so funny...

Chickens are so funny. If you have ever been on a farm, you know that they will follow you around everywhere you go. Why? Because they think you are going to feed them. I have been to farms where a rooster wanted to show who was the boss, only to change his mind and follow me because he thought I had something to eat. They can be quite comical.

I was at a small farm conference at which former NFL player Jason Brown was speaking at a breakfast. As I discussed in the previous chapter, the first thing that fascinated me about him was his career and the fact that he left the NFL to become a farmer at his prime. To me it said a lot about what his principles were and that they matter more to him than fame and fortune. He cares deeply about his family and his community. But when he went on to tell us about a story concerning his son, who was less than ten at the time, that spoke volumes to how he is raising his kids.

Jason put his son, who really wasn't interested at the time, in charge of the chickens. But Jason told him, "if you don't take care the chickens, they will tell on you." That kind of took his son off-guard but he moved on. Later his son started to get the meaning of what his father said, for if he didn't do his chores concerning the chickens, they did not produce eggs and thus they would "tell" on him. So, once he discovered taking care of the chickens was not a cakewalk and he would actually be held accountable for what he did or didn't do, he made sure he was getting his work done. Otherwise, the chickens would tell on him, just like his father said.

So things had been going well and his son wasn't missing a beat, until one day, the chickens were not producing eggs again. His father told him, "the chickens are telling on you." But his son was taken aback, because he was doing everything he was supposed to do. His father told him he'd want to investigate it because the chickens were telling on him, and he would have to figure it out.

After investigating the chicken house, his son discovered what was going on. He raced back to the house and told his dad, "I figured it out!" His face indicated that he had solved the crime of the century! With a big smile, he pointed out the steps he had taken, including searching around the chicken house. His investigation discovered a culprit that was eating the eggs. That's right – you may have guessed it. It was a black snake. And with him exclaiming his victory, he had the snake in his other hand to show his dad. The snake was as long as he was, but here he was holding it with no fear and living in victory!

Now, how often have the "chickens" told on you? Have they told on you in your business? You said you wanted it, you had great ideas and this was going to be the winner! But, you didn't follow through and do the work. You weren't consistent in the chores that would make you produce and often made excuses. Well guess what? The chickens are telling on you.

Often in farming, life lessons teach you more than a book. Without putting in the effort, you can't produce anything. This also goes for times you have problems. Sometimes there may be a proverbial snake keeping you from your goal. But once you know what the problem is, you can't allow it to stop you. You have a choice at every new road: Do something about the issues or put your head in the sand while the snake eats your eggs.

Are you willing to let this happen in your personal life and relationships? Or are these situations more important to you? Are you trying to get promoted at work but feel you are blocked? Is it the "snake" in you or another part of the process?

As always, it boils down to this: What are you going to do about it?

When I think of Mr. Brown's son grabbing a snake as long as he was and presenting it as a victory because he dealt with it, it makes me wonder, what haven't I dealt with that has been keeping me back? When you think to yourself, "I should be much further ahead" in whatever goal you set (marriage, finances, education, career, health), you have to ask yourself, what you are allowing to hold you back?

Not all of us are bold enough to grab the problem by the neck and face it. But why not? It is your life and you only get to live it once. Don't waste it. If you have come to the point that you recognize the snake but don't know how to get it out of your life, get help addressing it so you can win.

It is only those who have dealt with the adversity in life who ever live victoriously. Why not start today? Why not be the next success story who will build up someone else and inspire them to climb? Anyone who you admire due to their success has had to deal with the dilemmas of life. It is what they did to resolve them that changed things.

It would have been so much easier for Jason Brown's son to say, "I don't know what's going on and I did all I could" or "It's not my farm, I just did what you told me to do" or "It's not my fault."

But his son didn't make that choice, and we shouldn't either. This is one example where we readily should apply the saying paraphrased from Isaiah 11:6 from the Old Testement in the Bible: "A little child shall lead you." Do the hard thing so you can become the great thing. Otherwise the chickens will tell on you, and there will be no one to blame except yourself.

Chapter 4
Wisdom Mind vs. Emotional Mind

"Agriculture is our wisest pursuit, because it will in the end contribute most to real wealth, good morals, and happiness." –Thomas Jefferson

Shaolin Monks were Originally Farmers?!

| Yes! Shaolin Monks, world-famous for their incredible abilities in martial arts, were originally farmers. Marauders would steal from the monks. An Indian monk named Bodhidharma taught his fellow monks breathing exercises and helped them strengthen themselves. This lead to the creation of Shaoli Kung Fu.

Peril

Throughout time, knowledge has been passed down from generation to generation by family fireside chats, talking while working and learning, as well as other means. This chapter works from that principle but has been passed down through Chinese martial arts.

When we don't control our thoughts, our emotions take us in the wrong direction causing mistakes that bring peril. It is said in a self-defense situation, if you can control your Fear by looking at something properly, if you can control your Anxiety of dealing with a threat, if you can control the Time you have to deal with the situation, and last but not least, if you can control your Emotions in dealing with an issue, then you can control your F.A.T.E.

F.A.T.E. stands for Fear, Anxiety, Time, and Emotions.

Often in farming, like life, there are things you can control and things you can't. There are methods of doing things that can't take into account how you feel about them. They are necessary. When issues come, you can't panic and quit; you have to endure. As we said at the beginning, you are invested and committed.

So the question is, what do you do when your emotional mind floods in on you?

Do you turn to emotional thinking and possibly destroy the opportunity you have in your personal or business life? We will not always feel we are doing the best job, so we have to work on our feelings through coaching the mind and remembering that wisdom is not based on emotion.

Baguazhang is one of three Chinese internal martial arts. It is based on the theory of continuous change in response to a given situation. It is an internal form of traditional Moo Doe that sharpens reflexes and cultivates the understanding of one's mind and body.

In the book "Baguazhang: Emei Baguazhang Theory and Applications," there is a chapter that deals with the wisdom mind and emotional mind. The interesting thing about this chapter is we are often told the same information, but not necessarily in this way.

The book describes the wisdom mind as the analytical, technical, reasoning, instructional mind. This is the mind we use when we do math, technically learn how to play an instrument, or build something. It is necessary for problem-solving and resolution. It is something we use to manage and plan. The thing about the wisdom mind is it will

Remember that creating a successful marriage is like farming: You have to start over again every morning. -H. Jackson Brown, Jr.

SHAOLIN MONK FACTS

| THEY TRAIN IN THE USE OF 36 WEAPONS

| EACH MONK PICKS TWO ANIMAL MOVEMENTS AND STYLES IN WHICH TO SPECIALIZE

never lead you down the wrong path. You may not have all the information needed to resolve a problem, but it is resourceful enough to reach to out for the answers. The emotional mind allows us to express ourselves, be passionate, and be charitable. This is the mind that creates beauty in the world through art, music, and other mediums. Why is it that two people with the same classical instructional background playing the violin can sound completely different? Neither makes a mistake in the technical aspects of playing (wisdom mind) but one person makes it sound like it is alive and singing (emotional mind).

This is the secret of wisdom mind and emotional mind: you must use them as a team with each doing its job and applying the talents of the other when necessary. But, as we learn from life and farming, you can't be lead by your emotional mind because feelings and emotions change.

Let's look at a couple of examples. If you are passionate about helping people to become healthier and fit, you have to do more than be a cheerleader. You have to learn how to help them develop strength, increase fitness levels of cardio, learn proper nutrition, rest, and manage their time. These are all technical skills that have to be learned. But they started with an emotional thought to improve to themselves to which you applied wisdom in order to help them achieve their goal.

If you want a better relationship, you can't just think about how much you feel for someone. You have to look at how you are behaving with them, managing your time with them, and planning for the future. All these things are motivated by your emotions, but nothing is accomplished without a wisdom approach. For example, you may find that someone you know strengthens their relationship by taking short day trips with their spouse to keep things fresh, so you plan to do the same with your spouse.

Now let's look at how staying only in the emotional mind causes destruction.

Let's say you were concerned about how a client felt about your presentation and because you have not heard from them in two weeks, you go into a panic. You think to yourself, "they must have decided to work with someone else" or "they hated my presentation, what could I had done better," and the list goes on. Well, often when you act on the vacuum of thoughts, you may dampen your opportunities to be successful.

So let's say you act on your anxiety, you call the client too soon to check in and advise them about how you can provide further services. What did you just do? You diminished your impression in their eyes. They know you are hungry for their business and may negotiate the terms accordingly. They could also think that you don't have enough business and may not be successful enough to handle their accounts.

But the reality of it may have been that your client had a major change due to the legal climate which forced them to put your proposal on the back burner for

a bit. As soon as they could clear the air, they planned to implement your proposal. That is, until you called them too soon. Your anxiety got the best of you. Even if they are still collaborating with you, you may have lost respect in their eyes.

Have you ever worked for a boss or had a spouse or a best friend who had not been communicating with you and made you wonder what was going on? You thought about what you might have done wrong, and your emotional mind may lead you to say the wrong thing: To your boss, you might say, "I don't think you appreciate what I do around here." To your spouse, you might say, "I don't know what your problem is, but I work too hard and don't deserve the silent treatment." And to your best friend, you might say, "what is going on with you, you don't call, are you mad about something?"

Well, the reality might be that your boss is consumed by department changes and is trying to make sure the team is not impacted. Your spouse may be having health problems. And your best friend's father may be critically ill, causing them to be distracted. In all of these cases, you just made things worse by operating from your emotional mind and thinking the worst of your boss, spouse, and friend.

Consider that in all three situations, you could have stopped to use your wisdom mind in addressing what you were feeling emotionally. Using your wisdom mind, you could approach your boss and ask, "how are you doing, you have seen pretty busy lately." You could approach your spouse and ask, "you have seemed quieter than usual, how are things going in your world?" You could speak with your best friend and say, "we haven't spoken in a bit, so I thought I better check on you."

The outcome in these situations would be totally different just because you used your wisdom mind instead of your emotional mind.

Again, your wisdom mind should lead your decision making, but your emotional mind adds so much to others and the world around you. They each have a purpose which allows you to have a more effective and fulfilling life. So use them accordingly.

Chapter 5
Being Rooted

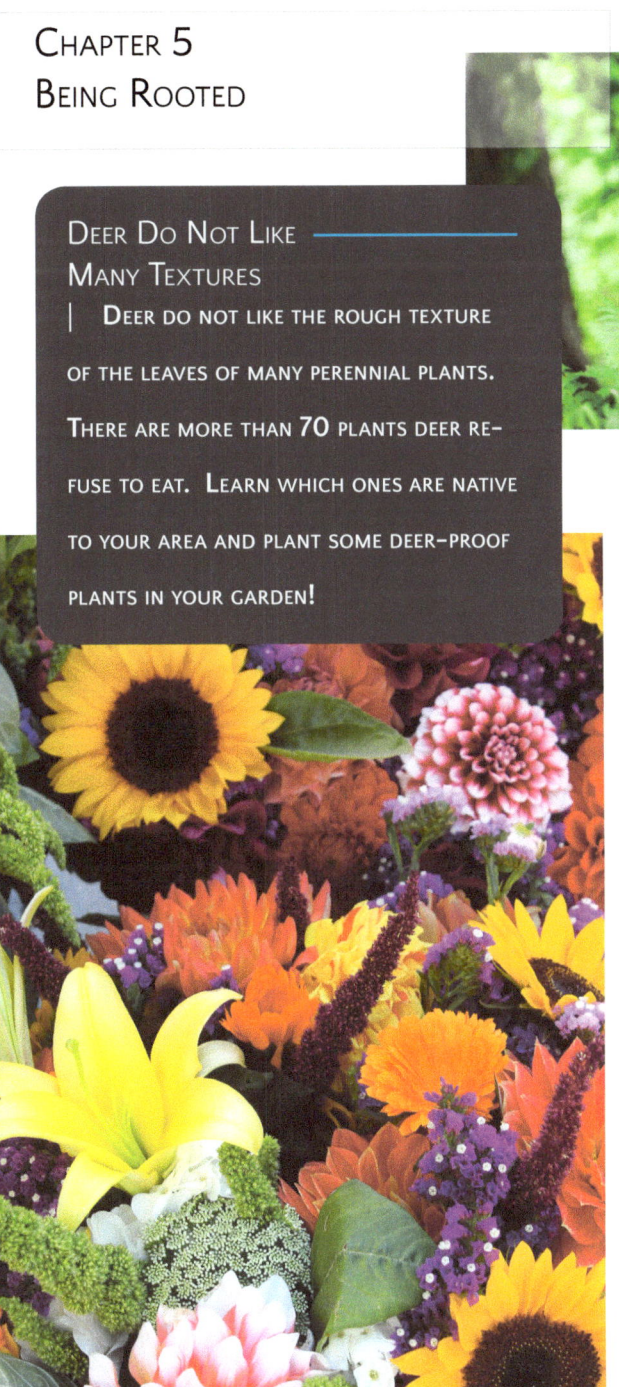

Deer Do Not Like Many Textures

Deer do not like the rough texture of the leaves of many perennial plants. There are more than 70 plants deer refuse to eat. Learn which ones are native to your area and plant some deer-proof plants in your garden!

What Gets You Up In The Morning?

Hummingbird Gardens is owned by Amanda Montgomery, who got her start in farming by volunteering at Tricycle Urban Ag Culture. Tricycle is Richmond, Virginia's leading urban agriculture nonprofit organization, working with urban farm deserts to support and educate the communities they serve about agriculture. Amanda went on to graduate school and also worked with a university farm. She found she would much rather be working outside. She continued to work with other small farms and some business and educational programs that inspired her to start her own farm program. She started with herbs and spices because it was different than the market. Then she started working with restaurants and partnered with other businesses. She expanded her business into fresh cut flowers. Now Amanda provides them to local companies and florists in her area. Her flowers are often seen at galas, weddings, and other social functions.

When asked what gets her up in the morning, Amanda said, "the morning is the best time. Harvesting in the morning when the birds are singing, the sun is rising, and having a full arm of flowers? It is the best." Her home is a certified wildlife habitat. She went on to say that seeing all of the life in her yard really inspires her. Observing the native bees and insects makes it really gratifying to positively impact the earth. Often, people walk by her yard and she is able to share information with them. Some people have been inspired by her and have created their own gardens of wild flowers and other items to improve their environment. The more flowers there are, the more sources insects have for nectar, and the happier pollinators (such as bees, butterflies, birds, etc.) are going to be. They will stick around and reproduce. This diverse environment attracts many different pollinators. She uses her greenhouse to control small plants in environments until they are able to be transplanted into her main gardens at various locations.

In this chapter, let us look at two things: The roots of our existence you can see, and the roots you can't. Well, when it comes to farming, it seems obvious that the roots you can't see are under the soil. But without soil teeming with life (insects, worms, microbes, bacteria, fungi, etc.), it can't produce further life. The same is true above ground. When the pollinators we spoke of earlier don't have a variety of plants from which to get nectar or cross-pollinate, we also have issues producing further life. So as you can see, it takes more than sunlight and water to produce a harvest. You have to ask, what impacts roots? When we speak of roots, we are not just speaking of the roots of plants, but how plants are part of the root system that sustains life.

Roots Below

With healthy soil, as stated above, full of life, you can create a strong root system to support the plant. Without healthy soil, you have run-off with the rain or water that may

come. This vital resource therefore cannot support the health and growth of the plant. Everything grows best in a vibrant environment.

Roots Above

As plants and flowers push their way through, pollinators thrive in a diverse environment and cross pollinate plant life. This is important because it totally impacts life on earth. You may say, that is a little melodramatic, but consider this: We depend on pollinators for 70% of the crops we eat. Some scientists have gone as far as to say humanity would last only four years without them because of their impact on food sources.

Now let's look at how this impacts us in personal growth.

We will discuss the internal (roots below) and external (roots above) that impact our ability to truly live with purpose in our lives. Much of this information is not new, but when was the last time you stopped to consider it?

Internal

How do you speak about yourself? How do you perceive people's opinions of you? How do you let someone's thoughts about you impact how you feel about yourself? Do you know your purpose in life? Have you identified your gifts, skills, and abilities? Do you know what you are capable of? What types of people are speaking to you in your life? Are they going in the same direction you want or are they holding you back? Are you doing self-development? Do you have mentors?

All of these things impact your ability to have healthy mental soil that reaps a harvest, but it doesn't work without attention.

External

Are you watching trends (the way farmers watch the weather) to see direction in relationships, your career, and your health? If you aren't watching and responding, you are being swept away and finding yourself reacting versus being proactive. This impacts the number of divorces, friendships lost, business and industry failures, sickness, obesity statistics, and the like. We have to keep pushing forward with our purpose. We also have to support it with our lifestyle of fitness, nutrition, communication in relationships, and constantly learning about industry and business.

What types of people are robbing you and your energy? Are they like deer or voles? Are you operating in toxic environments? Are you drained after dealing with people? Are you doing work that inspires you and is rewarding?

In order to create a massive harvest, we have to look at, take action with, and review our plans to win.

If you say to yourself, "it doesn't take all that", you are cutting yourself short. Everything that has life was created to produce.

You can't have activity below ground or above ground that destroys your ability to produce. But, you must be constant and vigilant in looking at your world. If you don't know what is going on, everything else will shape your world, including your harvest.

So what are you going to do?

It has been said, if it is important to you, you find a way. If not, you will find an excuse!

Last but not least, "You can make things better or you can make things worse, it is up to you"-Zig Ziglar

Chapter 6
The Potential Is In The Seed

Drones

| Farmers are relying on drones now more than ever.
| This includes:
| Soil and field analysis
| Planting
| Crop spraying
| Crop monitoring
| Irrigation
| Health assessment

Don't judge each day by the harvest you reap but by the seeds that you plant. −Robert Louis Stevenson

In The Bag

During a farm conference I attended at Virginia State University, I observed a drone demonstration that gave farmers a birds-eye view of their fields. They could see plants damaging their crops, flooded areas, and more. The scans from the drone allowed them to analyze the information and be able to act on it.

Afterward the demonstration, I spoke with Bob Waring of Brandon Farms in Newport News, Virginia, whose field we were watching on video.

He said, "the most potential is seeds in the bag". In other words, it is what happens after the seeds come out of the bag that affects them. Before the seeds come out of the bag, there is no contamination. Once they are out of the bag, they can be exposed to many things and become corrupted by disease and by their environment.

He went on to say the job of a farmer was to take all the stress away from the plant and let it do its job. We went on to discuss little organisms and big rain. This is to say, that the soil is teeming with little organisms that have a greater potential in producing for the plant, while big rain helps to flourish the plant. This speaks to another fact about teeming life in the soil. When big rain comes to the wrong soil, and the plant is surrounded by life, it will

cause erosion and take away what life and nutrients are there. On the other hand, with the right soil, when big rain comes, what the soil can't handle is absorbed by the rest of the life around it. This allows it to flourish and, as Bob said, "do its job".

One example of this in our lives is when someone has an addiction and they don't have a supportive environment that allows them to deal with challenges. If people are in a supportive environment, then a positive community of friends, family, and professionals can enrich their lives.

When you ponder what Bob said, you can't help but think of self development and raising children.

How often have you been in the wrong field or environment that didn't make you flourish?

What type of life was choking you out or hindering your progress?

Did you have the right little organisms of support or mentoring?

When the big rains came, did you allow yourself to be washed away? Or did you connect with people who could help you sustain the storm?

What will you do differently in the future?

Whether you are an entrepreneur, work in a corporation, or have another type of occupation, we all have to deal with the environment that we plant ourselves in. But, you also have to live like the drone. Step away sometimes from that birds-eye view and evaluate: Is this going in the right direction for me? Is the soil supporting where I want to go? Are there weeds or plants growing into my crop that I have to either work with or remove?

Well, sometimes you to have the liberty to remove the weeds and plants in your field, and sometimes you don't. But even if you don't, that doesn't mean you don't evaluate things. You have to evaluate the impact and make some decisions.

At the same field day farm conference, I observed analysis from a drone scan. It showed that morning glory plants were growing in a segment of their crops. After taking the time to analyze what was going on, the decision had to be made on what to do about it. In this particular case, they allowed the morning glories to continue growing because they wouldn't have a large impact on the yield of the crop, but removing them would.

That brings us to the next part of the seed/plant analogy related to our lives that comes to mind: Child development.

Every child comes into this world with potential, but it is the environment that the child comes up in that shapes their impact on the world. If you take Bob's advice about removing the stress from the plant, it will do what it was meant to do, and this syncs with a child. Just like farming, parenting takes patience, being flexible, and being resourceful according to parent, coach, and positive discipline educator Meganne Ford of Be Kind Coaching in Richmond, Virginia.

Just like unhealthy soil (versus life-enriched soil), we often fill the void we feel in our lives with things that tear us down. We have not planted the seed and given someone the empowering choice to pick someone up and start over. This applies to children and adults alike.

But with a child, like the morning glories, we have to look at the process of what is going on versus just the product. In the morning glory example, the farmer allowed the plants to stay by analyzing what their impact would be on the crop. Often, as parents we don't show the patience and flexibility to look at the process for the child. We often just want to make sure we have the end product of what the child should be. The risk in this, as Meganne told me, is there is so much development that goes on in the process.

Have you ever seen a picture from your child and had no idea what they were presenting? Or you went to a child's school and saw the artwork on the board and wondered, possibly with disappointment, "why didn't Jimmy's work look as good as Jane's?" Were you looking at the product or the process? Were you horrified by the "morning glories" and the threat to your "product"? Or could you pull back and see their imperfections were part of the learning process and not a threat? The process of learning motor skills and expression through drawing, using scissors, or making pictures with sticks is part of the process. It will allow a child to produce their best product down the road.

Another concept Meganne Ford discussed was safe fails.

In business, we often want to jump the gun at stopping a process if it isn't yielding the results we want right away, like marketing. But often we have to follow through and learn from our experience in order to see where it goes and analyze the result. In child development as well as self-development with a mentor, this is called a safe fail. Let's look at an example that Meganne gave me which occurred when her niece was much younger.

Her niece was spending time with her and they were going to Subway® to get dinner. Meganne told her, yes we can go, but you will have to order for yourself. So they went in and her niece ordered a meatball sub. They asked her what she wanted on it and she said mayo. The server was shocked and it took Meganne off-guard as well. The server repeatedly asked her if she was sure that was what she wanted and she said yes. Meganne went on to tell the server, "you heard the lady, give her what she wants".

They went home and when they pulled out their sandwiches, her niece realized that while she asked for mayo on her sandwich, what she meant to say was that she wanted cheese. Meganne told her she didn't have to eat it, but they were not going back to the store. Her niece scraped the mayo off the bun and went on to eat her meatball sub. Because Meganne allowed this to happen, her niece had the courage to make orders at other restaurants while her girlfriends weren't comfortable doing it. A safe fail helped her niece in her development. The safe fail didn't destroy her life but improved it.

Also, Meganne helped her to step up by asking her to order for herself while knowing she could not truly injure herself in doing so. When her niece made a mistake in ordering, she could only learn from it. In this way, we have the ability to shape each other's lives as parents, mentors, business owners, and in other leadership positions. We have to be able to be flexible, patient, and resourceful. This is how we bring the seed along on its journey to become what it was meant to be.

As was pointed out earlier, when you don't fill this void with teaching lessons, someone or something else will. Is that what you want?

Last but not least, when we look at the potential of the seed, consider this: Don't spend all of your time trying not to fail but rather be able to adjust, to deal with mistakes, bad results, and dilemmas. Someone once said the road to success is full of failing large and failing fast. Once you have, your development will propel you to the next level of success. If you only play it safe, you will only win small. No matter what you do in life, what you do impacts the people you serve, work for, and work with. Be aware of how you impact the soil of your environment. Are you enriching it or making it weaker? Every life is a seed and you impact its potential by how you live.

Chapter 7
Why Did I Start Farming?

The Mindset...

Entrepreneurs and farmers both know there is no "plan B." Even when you can't see results yet, you have to commit to your plan if you want to receive a harvest. Be committed to finding out what you're doing and address it.

Meaningful Living

A couple of chapters ago we met Amanda Montgomery who said that her introduction to farming changed her life, gave her purpose, and made her life more meaningful as she helped others through her work. It gave her freedom, yet made her commit to her vision in order to grow. Like Amanda, the owners of Broadfork Farm in Chesterfield, Virginia, had similar beginnings.

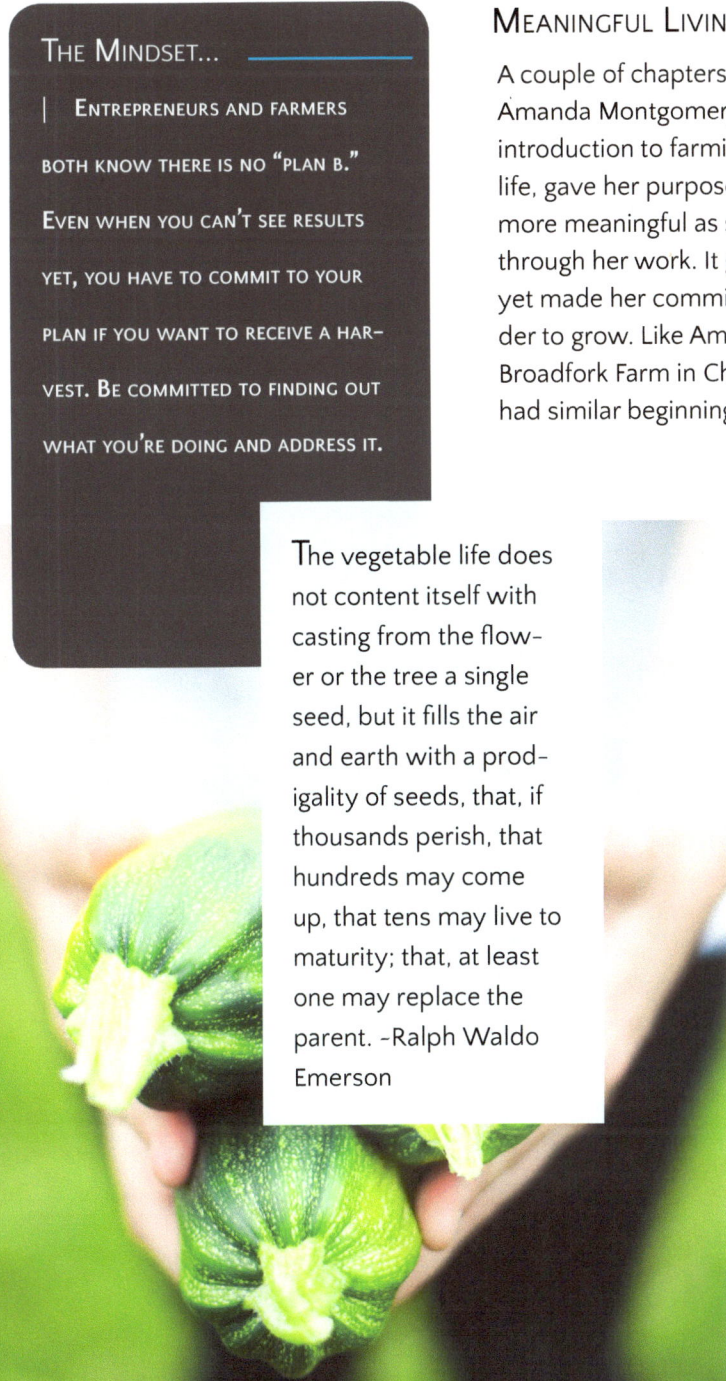

The vegetable life does not content itself with casting from the flower or the tree a single seed, but it fills the air and earth with a prodigality of seeds, that, if thousands perish, that hundreds may come up, that tens may live to maturity; that, at least one may replace the parent. -Ralph Waldo Emerson

How did two college students with degrees in Biology from David and Lafayette Colleges, as well as one who earned a Master's Degree in Education from the Harvard Graduate School of Education, end up as farming entrepreneurs? Janet Aardema and Dan Gagnon applied their education to use in farming and to share their passion for farm education.

33

Here is how Janet described their journey:

"My introduction to farming was being introduced to multiple small-scale, diversified, organic vegetable farms in the Pacific Northwest after moving to that area in my early twenties. I started this farm business because of my love for being surrounded by food growing in the ground, my love for working in the soil, and my desire to do the good work of growing really nutritious food for my community. Fortunately, all of these reasons are also the reasons I keep farming, despite the challenges. The additional reason that has kept me farming is the incredible, superb flavor of the food we grow compared to our options if we weren't farming. For my family as well as the community members that this farm feeds, there is constant feedback that the food tastes so incredibly delicious! Care and attention to the biological life of the soil is a critically important component of farming.

Healthy soil is what supports us all, and in order to be healthy, soil needs to be alive, diverse, and have an active community of interacting organisms. This is the natural way of soil in a wild, undisturbed setting. In order for soil to maintain these properties in a cultivated (farmed) setting, we the farmers need to constantly be mindful of feeding the soil and promoting a diverse and thriving community of micro-organisms. This is the only way to grow healthy and nutritious plants and thus support healthy humans through the production of nutritious food. My deep relationship with our community due to this farm is amazingly important. The community support makes our farm possible, both financially and spiritually. For me, farming is too hard to continue without a direct relationship with the community members who love this food. Our farm is successful due to Dan's and my strong and productive partnership, our willingness to work very hard and for many hours, and our insistence in researching deeply the most likely strategies for success."

As with most success stories, we may look at Janet and Dan, believing their climb to success was overnight. We don't see the development, the failure, the opportunities missed, and the humble beginnings. Some people don't realize the journey farmers have to make to have a sustainable and successful farm. Farming is no different than any other business; it takes hustle and determination. You work hard to produce and you work hard to market to the people who want your products. It is not as easy as growing something and throwing a shingle up that says, "Fresh produce for sale."

Like any entrepreneurial venture, talent or a product is not enough; you have to learn and manage the business. This is where many people fail. They don't seek training and advice. Instead, they go at it like a lone wolf.

That is an interesting thing about farmers: at every conference, visit or interview, everyone was willing to share with me what they know. So often the problem for entrepreneurs is that they don't seek help. By seeking help and gaining knowledge through training and certifications, you highly increase your opportunity for success.

In Virginia, as in many states, there may be a cooperative extension which teaches everything from soil development to financial management and marketing. There are classes, seminars, conferences, certifications, and all other aspects of agribusiness. This support is crucial to a farmer's success.

Why is it so important to invest in your business? Because you didn't get started to quit. As an entrepreneur, you will have great obstacles to overcome, so you had better be pretty strong. You will also have to develop a "no matter what" attitude which includes life balance. For example, you can't neglect your family just to make it in your career. You have to make them part of your "why" commitment or contract.

But as always, you have to remember to ask yourself why you are doing what you are doing to stay in check. The farmers I spoke with for this book span from married with no children and only one being involved in farming to a family of four children with the husband and wife not only building the business but home schooling their children as well. For farms of any size, however, it is a large undertaking dependent on their commitment to blocking time for work, family support, and structure. So many entrepreneurs and career-oriented people have not learned this balance, which often leads to damaged relationships. These relationships are often strained or ruined because of a lack of communication and balance. I point all of these things out because when all the chips are down, having a strong support system and a great "why" makes the difference of being a success versus quitting and burning bridges in relationships.

So what is the difference in this dedication if you want to be an entertainer, a CEO, a restaurant owner, a politician, an athlete, etc.? Absolutely nothing! In all these situations, you are either building something externally for yourself as an entrepreneur or internally within an organization for a career. The interesting thing about working in a career is you have the opportunity to have an impact and move up to a level of success. So you are operating as a business in a business, because you have to mind your business to build a career! You cannot look at yourself just as an employee because you want something larger.

Let's look at some of those farming activities that lead to success.

Planning

Planning covers so many things in farming. If I'm just starting, what do I have that is viable? What knowledge do I have about what I plan to do with farming? Is this a hobby or a profession? If it is a profession, what do I need to know that will make me competitive in the market?

What will be the time needed on my investment before I see a return? How do I continue to build on this return? Who do I need on my team to make this successful (mentors, labor, instructors, CPA, attorney, suppliers, market access, etc)? You must consider this and more before you have broken ground to plant the first seed or purchased the first livestock or equipment. How often do we take the time to plan? Sometimes we are fortunate enough to find someone along the way who lets us know we are off course. Then we still have to determine if we are going to listen.

Let's look at several examples where this makes the difference.

People Who Want to Lose Weight and Keep It Off

A person says to themselves, "I can do this and if I just don't eat, I'll lose weight." In the beginning it works, and the pounds come off. Then they get to a plateau and can't move any further. Now, they may have achieved their weight loss goal and they're pretty excited. So they return to their former lifestyle and gain the weight back.

Have you ever known someone who dieted and did this? It happens all the time. We look for a quick fix but boomerang and our weight comes back, sometimes more than before, which often leads to more issues. No one told you you were slowing your metabolism down. No one told you that you were stripping your body of the nutrients you needed. No one taught you how to form a nutritional plan that you could live by long-term. No one taught you strengthening the body burns calories and helps to maintain lean muscle mass, while reducing body fat. No one told you that the proper amount of quality rest and adequate water were vital to keeping the body balanced and healthy.

Now the real question is, "Did no one tell you or did you not bother to ask?"

Two Professional Mixed Martial Arts Fighters Trying to Reach the Top

One fighter is naturally talented with good movement, reflexes, and striking ability. He knows how to work hard. He gets up early, he runs, he is in the gym doing bag work, conditioning with jump ropes, and has the same sparring partner that he started with. He starts out of the blocks winning every fight with timing and speed using his knock-out strikes. But as time goes on, he can't seem to get to the next level: Why?

The second fighter has watched other fighters make the climb and asked, "what did it take to get where you are?" He discovers his talent will only get him so far, so he starts asking for help and doing the work. He trains with various coaches for striking, conditioning, ground, sparring, nutrition, and strategy. These coaches bring him to the next level through development. He becomes the champion, not just because of natural ability, but the fighter's determination to find out what he didn't know and apply it.

Two College Graduates Starting in a Company with the Goal of Climbing the Ladder

Both graduates are bright, both are hard working, and both want to get to the highest levels of management and possibly become CEO or president.

One believes that if they do an awesome job, their work with speak for itself, and they will rise. And to a certain extent, they do. They start in an entry level position and continue to develop their technical abilities. They move up for years and show their skills to be of benefit to the company. They are often called to assist in training others. But somehow, they are not being looked at for management.

The second one starts off the same as the first, but since their long-term interest is to rise to higher levels in their career, they start asking questions about the culture. They start networking to learn more about the people who are already at or above the levels they wish to achieve. They read books on leadership and business systems and invest even further in their self-development. They gain mentors to whom they have demonstrated their abilities. Then these mentors connect them to further opportunities to shine and to their network. As the years go on, with gained responsibility and a track record for leading, developing, and mentoring others, they are given the opportunity to become a Vice President, while still working towards their goal of becoming CEO or President.

What was the element in all of these examples?

Planning.

And this is only the first step in life success, whether it is as an individual, athlete, entrepreneur, career or other area. You will have to plan to win. Planning is key, but don't forget the other areas that will determine your success. In our lives, like farming, we have to execute action by putting in the right work. There is a difference between the right work and just work. In this chapter, you saw many examples of people who worked hard but didn't get the results they wanted. So we must execute the right action, do maintenance, review it, allow the fields to recover, etc., and start planning again.

Chapter 8
Allowing the Fields to Recover

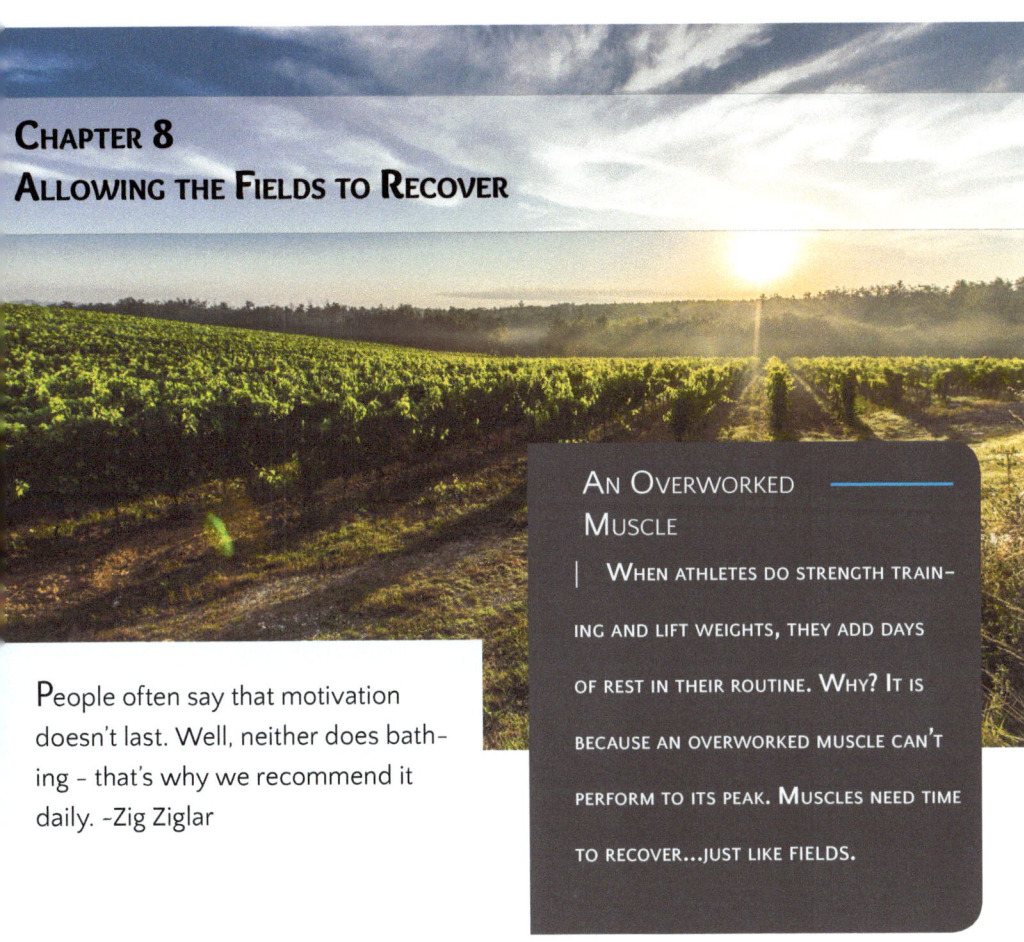

People often say that motivation doesn't last. Well, neither does bathing - that's why we recommend it daily. -Zig Ziglar

An Overworked Muscle

When athletes do strength training and lift weights, they add days of rest in their routine. Why? It is because an overworked muscle can't perform to its peak. Muscles need time to recover...just like fields.

Recovery Time

In farming, you have to rotate crops in order to allow field to recover. Why?

Crop rotation is the process of growing different types of crops (or none at all) in the same area over a sequence of seasons. Historians believe crop rotation in farming was developed as early as 6,000 B.C., and that it was started in the Middle East.

Without rotating crops, your yields decrease over the years. The land becomes tired and less fertile because nutrients are drained. Pests increase in number since the same crops remain their home. There is a higher risk of erosion, and the list goes on.

So what do you do? Well, different crops need different nutrients from soil. A variety of crops allows the land to remain nutrient-rich or fertile. But if you don't plant anything and leave the fields to recover for a period of time, they will replenish and restore their nutrients.

Now here is the kicker. Farmers found that crop rotation helped to increase productivity and planting different crops replenished the soil nutrients. The alternation fought erosion and made the soil stable. And remember when we discussed pests? Well, crop rotation eliminated their regular food source.

This takes some planning, but it is highly effective for productivity.

So, the questions are:

How often do you allow the "fields" of your mind to recover? Have you learned to shutdown and plan for recovery the same way you plan for your goals? Exercise is an excellent example of how this works. You can actually get stronger by working a muscle hard one day and then letting it recover. Weight loss, like business (believe it or not), requires adequate rest to make sure your body stays in balance to achieve goals. Do you rotate activity to allow yourself a fresh outlook at your goals and life? Do you go to seminars, travel for new experiences that enrich your life, or take a trip to tell yourself, "this is why I dedicate the time I do to my goals"?

Do you keep doing the same thing, but find it is not producing the same results, or has diminishing returns? Does this sound like you are looking at life from the treetops or are you caught in the forest dealing with the rat race of being busy?

Are you burning out? Are there adequate nutrients in the "fields" of your mind so you can develop what you want and need to grow?

Have you had the same mindset for so long that the "pests" of your mind and the environment are robbing you of the success you want and need?

There are two sayings we can look at related to this. One saying is that a dull axe cuts nothing. The second saying is that you'll hardly reach any higher than your closest five friends. Both of these sayings deal with the "pests" of your mind.

Consider this: If you work harder and longer without a refresher and your mental "axe" dulls, and you tell yourself, "I don't have time for a break, I have to get it done no matter what", what are you really accomplishing?

But the most important question is, what is the real cost of your dulled mental "axe"? It could be your health, your relationships, your mind, and even your goals. We have to show wisdom and be around people who are successful and who have learned from their mistakes or avoided them because of a mentor's advice.

With the other saying, "you'll hardly reach higher than your closest five friends," this doesn't mean that you get rid of them, because good friends are hard to find. But you must move in circles of the "eagles" who are going in the direction you are trying to reach. A lot of people see this in business, but often they do not look at it in their personal life. If your friends always have excuses for why their lives are the way they are and feel justified in their resolve, they have just decided to stay in a stagnant existence. This is not growth, and you can't be healthy physically or mentally, or be inspired to be a better you, in this environment. You must remove the "pests" of your life by rotating into different fields, planting a different crop, and sometimes allowing the soil to be fallow by removing yourself from an unhealthy environment and letting things recover. Pests like their environment to stay the same, so they can build a stronger home for what they like. Therefore, change and growth are key!

If we don't take care of our fields, no one will. We have to pay attention to not only what we need, but plan for it in the future like we plan everything else. Don't leave this out or you will be left wondering what happened to your fields - also known as your life!

Chapter 9
It's Time for Market

Bringing it all to market...

What Have We Learned?

Well, throughout this book you have planned, planted, cultivated, weeded out, raised, and prepared. It is time for market!

There are so many things you have done, worked through, suffered, survived, and conquered in yourself and with your product to get to this point. How does it feel? Do you feel you are offering your best? Do you wish you had accomplished more? Do you have regrets because you didn't have the harvest you hoped for?

Farmers Markets vs. Community Supported Agriculture

Both farmers markets and community supported agriculture, or CSAs, bring farmers and consumers together to sell and buy fresh produce. Farmers markets are seasonal, however, whereas CSAs provide produce year-round. Farmers markets are usually in the same place, but CSAs usually have 3-4 pickup places.

Even after everything, this is the best you have. That is the question and the solution. This is the best you have, right now! So don't bring it to market with regret because you have created a harvest and it is from the fruit of your labor. Never belittle your accomplishments. Never question yourself on comparisons, only evaluate. Why? Because if someone had a better result in their harvest, you could learn from it. You could master a new method, gain a skill, or develop an understanding that will increase your future harvest.

Think about what you bring to market. It is a product of you!

Since it is you, provide it with the utmost pride and serve it with excellence and zeal. Promote it as the finest you have to offer knowing what you are offering is your best.

People love coming to a farmers market because they know they are getting freshly grown products. Nothing is processed, and everything is made nature's way. They trust and have formed relationships with the people from whom they buy their produce. It is truly from "harvest to hand," as they say.

Now, not all products and produce made on the farm go directly to the farmers market. Some products are sold to restaurants because they want fresh produce or flowers for their business and meals. Some may be sold to larger companies for products that use their produce as an ingredient to another product, and the list goes on. The main point is, what you accomplished in your harvest is needed and you have a responsibility to give your best. Anything less, lessens all of us.

This is the same for our lives. Each of us is the result of our life experiences, training, developed abilities, and skills. What we bring to market makes an impact, not just in our lives and ability to survive, but also in the way we change the world around us. It is what we give the world.

There is no such thing as not making an impact in life. If you do nothing, your failure to do something makes an impact. It allows a vacuum to pull into place something less valuable because you didn't bother.

When you do something to make an impact, the quality and thoughtfulness of what you do has a bearing on the impact you make.

Are you giving your best? Are you growing? Are you learning? Are you sharing what you have learned?

Let's look at the nature of what you bring to market in some of the examples discussed earlier.

Harvest to Hand

An example of this would be a farmer who brings artisan breads to market. The breads have no preservatives, nothing artificial, and are just wholesome, fresh, and better for you. Or someone selling lotions and soaps made from goat's milk at the farmers market and demonstrating how their products work with the body naturally. You can see how their skills made the difference in what you received as the final product.

When someone is able to see what you bring with your blood, sweat, and tears, they have a stronger appreciation for it. They can relate better and you have the opportunity to have the highest impact. These are the people who trust that you have their best interest at heart. Your words or produce cause you to be a trusted root in their lives. This includes all relationships where you are a trusted resource.

Businesses You Support

The businesses you support have multiple meanings. It could be that what you provide teaches someone a better way of being and through this knowledge they impact others. It can also accent what the business does by making it superior in the customer's eyes to others because they are stronger for it. Let's use an example of someone giving a gift of flowers grown locally in their area. The business buys the flowers from the local grower. Because of the quality of the fresh, local flowers, the sales at the business increase because everyone wants them. The customer buying the flowers has a strong appreciation for the quality of the product. The person for whom they are buying the flowers has appreciation for the customer's thoughtfulness and the beauty of the fresh cut flowers. It is not as simple as being behind the scenes. What you do will shine through whether you are recognized for it or not. And with some businesses, they will want to highlight you because of your importance to their success.

Quiet Participation Can Still Mean a Large Impact

In Scottsburg, Virginia, Chandler's Gardens grows peppers and onions for a salsa company. People who buy the salsa have no idea who grew the ingredients.

Similarly, no one may know your name, but your influence is still felt. Why? Because you were part of the process. You are a necessary piece of the pie (or salsa), the dynamics, or the formula.

Another reason to care about what you bring to market? It is not just about you. It is about all the people you impact throughout your life. Whether you do it in your family, on the job, as an entrepreneur, as a teacher, or as the head of a company, we all have a responsibility to look at what we bring and make and what it took to get it there. This way we can appreciate what we have, remember who and what we are working for, and what we have to give.

In all you do, use your wisdom mind in decision making and stay rooted.

Know the potential of every seed you plant in the lives of others.

Have a strong "why" to keep you in the game that will make you determined to succeed no matter what.

Live in a balanced way and know the importance of allowing your fields to recover.

And know that what you bring to market is a reflection of you. When you don't strive for your best and do the right things it will reflect in your results, and THE CHICKENS WILL TELL ON YOU!!!

REFERENCES

Page 5 - "14 Celebrities Who Grew Up on Farms," Ranker.com, https://www.ranker.com/list/celebrities-who-grew-up-on-farms/celebrity-lists

Pages 9-12 - Wikipedia, s.v. "Jason Brown (American Football)" last modified June 14, 2018, 7:14 UTC, https://en.wikipedia.org/wiki/Jason_Brown_(American_football)

Lautner Farms, "Why a Star Football Player Traded NFL Career for Tractor," November 16, 2014, https://www.lautnerfarms.com/why-a-star-football-player-traded-nfl-career-for-a-tractor/

Page 10 - Photo from Twitter, https://twitter.com/wisefarmerbrown

Page 11 - Photo by Jamie Jones Photography, https://www.focusonthefamily.com/marriage/daily-living/jason-brown-from-the-nfl-to-farming

Page 18 - Shou-yu, Liang; Jwing-Ming, Yang; Wen-Ching, Wu. "Baguazhang: Emei Baguazhang Theory and Applications." Ymaa Publication Center; 2nd edition, 1996.

Page 23 - Smith, Lauren "10 Deer-Resistent Plants for Your Garden," House Beautiful. April 28, 2016. https://www.housebeautiful.com/lifestyle/gardening/g3470/deer-resistant-plants/

Page 27 - Mazur, Michal. "Six Ways Drones Are Revolutionizing Agriculture," MIT Technology Review. July 20, 2016. https://www.technologyreview.com/s/601935/six-ways-drones-are-revolutionizing-agriculture/

Page 37 - Wikipedia, s.v. "Mixed Martial Arts" last modified July 7, 2018, 23:20 (UTC), https://en.wikipedia.org/wiki/Mixed_martial_arts

Subway® and the Subway® logo are registered trademarks and service marks owned and registered by Subway IP Inc.

Quotes throughout the book are from the Brainy Quote website, https://www.brainyquote.com/.

Cover photo from www.canva.com. All other photos are from Pixabay (https://pixabay.com/) or from Pexels (https://www.pexels.com/) Illustrations by Jared Mason

Author Mark Winn

Mark Winn is a student of life and enjoys people. The results of his experience lead him to write about life lessons from clients, farmers & family.

https://www.facebook.com/ChickensTalkings/

www.ingramcontent.com/pod-product-compliance
Lightning Source LLC
Chambersburg PA
CBHW061049090426
42740CB00002B/85